DO I?

Questions to Answer Before You Say "I Do"

JANICE J. BURTON

www.TrueVinePublishing.org

Do I? Questions to Answer Before You Say "I Do"
By Janice J. Burton

Published by True Vine Publishing Company
P.O. Box 22448
Nashville, TN 37202
www.TrueVinePublishing.org

ISBN: 978-1-7357540-4-8

All scripture quotations taken from the Holy Bible, New International Version, unless otherwise noted.

Printed in the United States of America—First Printing

To place orders for more books or to book the author for speaking engagements, visit: www.DoItheBook.com

IN MEMORY

This book is dedicated to my Mother:
Mrs. Lela Mae Johnson

God chose her to give me life, and I honor her memory and legacy. She was a writer but in 96 years of life never owned a typewriter or computer. Everything was handwritten and continued until her hands were no longer steady. I was inspired by cards and letters to family and when I saw bibles and books in her bed as she studied and wrote sermons, speeches, and letters.

Mom: I miss you and love you. I know you're leaning over the balcony of heaven reading this book and cheering me on. I love you!

ACKNOWLEDGEMENTS

I have many people to thank and wish I could list everyone by name. If you fall in the category of family or friend, I am truly grateful for the love and support you give me always!

First and foremost, God: You are my everything! Thank you for stirring up the gift in me and for your presence every step of the way. Without you I am nothing, but through you, I can do all things!

To my anchor, my son, Michael, for your heart and loving care. To my wonderful siblings: Lonnie, Maxine, Theresa, Freddi, Rosalind, and Gary and to other family members for your love, support, and always spoiling me. You are my treasure!

To my accountability group: Leticia, Lois, Pat, and Tamara. Thank you for your motivation, support, and traveling this journey with me. I am grateful to Anita, Kimya, and Jennifer (JP) who literally cheered me along the way!

I thank my Delta Sorors, Nashville posse, Austin crew, Yadas, and Atlanta Thriving Tribe for your love, encouragement, and support. You know who you are. Thank you, Antonio, for the True Vine connection-you were a God-send!

True Vine Publishing: Wow! I learned so much through your guidance. I appreciate your kindness, professionalism, and support for making my first book a success!

To God Be The Glory!

TABLE OF CONTENTS

INTRODUCTION

I love weddings! They are beautiful, cherishable events and even breathtaking at times. We all have attended weddings and heard those famous words, "**I Do**" - simple, yet significant to confirm the sacred vows and solidify the marriage. That quick moment of "**I Do**" and exchange of vows is surely when hearts melt, faces smile, and tears drop as the couple prepares to whisk away happily to their forever after.

I absolutely love the idea of the whisk to happily ever after. That is what should happen and is ideal. Many couples can certainly attest to happy, lasting marriages. However, there is another reality: marriage is not quick like that "**I Do**" moment. Marriage is for a lifetime and will encompass moments of love and joy but also heartache and pain. Being in love does not automatically produce perfection or override life's realities, and couples will face many obstacles to fulfilling the vows. Yes, planning for the wedding is exciting, but planning for the marriage should be the priority. Marriage planning involves self-assessment and crucial discussions of how situations will be handled as a unit. It establishes roots from which couples should grow together.

I have written this book to help couples think beyond the wedding, butterflies, and fantasies. It is a compilation of questions starting with "**Do I?**" designed for introspection and diving into the spirit and soul in order to examine the decision to marry and willingness to put in the work.

I encourage each partner to first read the book individually and then later together. Take the time to meditate and reflect on the questions. Go deeper than "yes" or "no" - dissect the questions for in depth discussion and planning. Be honest, thoughtful, and respectful, even if some answers cause uneasiness. Have fun and be creative. There are scripture references for each chapter, so use the book for devotion or dating time.

If you are married or in a committed arrangement, this book is a great tool to assist you in reassessing your commitment and to boost the relationship to higher levels of life and love together.

CHAPTER 1

SPIRITUAL

Covenant

Spiritual Beliefs

Vision

You are God's creation, a created spirit. God divinely gave you a soul and put you in a body, but your spirit is who you are. This chapter deals with spiritual connectedness in the relationship. Pray for an open spirit and heart.

SCRIPTURE REFERENCES:

Genesis 2:18–24

18) The Lord God said, "It is not good for the man to be alone. I will make a helper suitable for him." 19) Now the Lord God had formed out of the ground all the wild animals and all the birds in the sky. He brought them to the man to see what he would name them, and whatever the man called each living creature, that was its name. 20) So the man gave names to all the livestock, the birds in the sky and all the wild animals. But for Adam no suitable helper was found. 21) So the Lord God caused the man to fall into a deep sleep; and while he was sleeping, he took one of the man's ribs and then closed up the place with flesh. 22) Then the Lord God made a woman from the rib he had taken out of the man, and he brought her to the man. 23) The man said, "This is now bone of my bones and flesh of my flesh; she shall be called 'woman,' for she was taken out of man." 24) That is why a man leaves his father and mother and is united to his wife, and they become one flesh.

Mark 10:9

9) Therefore what God has joined together, let no one separate.

COVENANT:

Covenant is a word we do not hear in everyday language. It is mostly associated with the Bible, ancient life, and how God made covenants as acts of divine promise. The sanctity of covenant goes deeper than love and commitment. It is an agreement, a vow, a sacred bond, and a solemn promise that *cannot* be broken.

Answer and Discuss.

Do I trust God to choose my mate?

Do I trust God's timing for the wait?

Do I know that God has chosen my mate for me?

Spend extra time with these questions. Spend as much time needed in prayer and communion with God for His guidance and answer. Trust God. (Proverbs 3:5,6...Trust in the Lord with all your heart, and do not lean to your own understanding. In all your ways acknowledge Him, and He will direct your path).

Do I know and understand that I am entering into a sacred, covenant agreement with God first and then with my mate to lovingly exist for a lifetime in a covenant relationship that I will not break and that divorce is not an option?

What thoughts do I have about covenant commitment?

Do I know that I am ready for a covenant relationship with my mate? Why?

If God left a small part of me incomplete, would my mate complete me?

Do I know that spiritual, emotional, and physical infidelities are not options?

Write your thoughts about dealing with temptation in these areas. Spiritual infidelity is putting the needs of your religion/church/ministry before the needs of your mate/children.

Do I understand the importance of sacrifice in a relationship?

Think about your mindset, habits, and characteristics that must change or be deleted in order to honor sacrifice in the relationship.

COVENANT — WHAT IS OUR PLAN?

_____

_____

_____

_____

_____

_____

_____

_____

_____

_____

_____

_____

_____

_____

_____

_____

_____

_____

_____

_____

_____

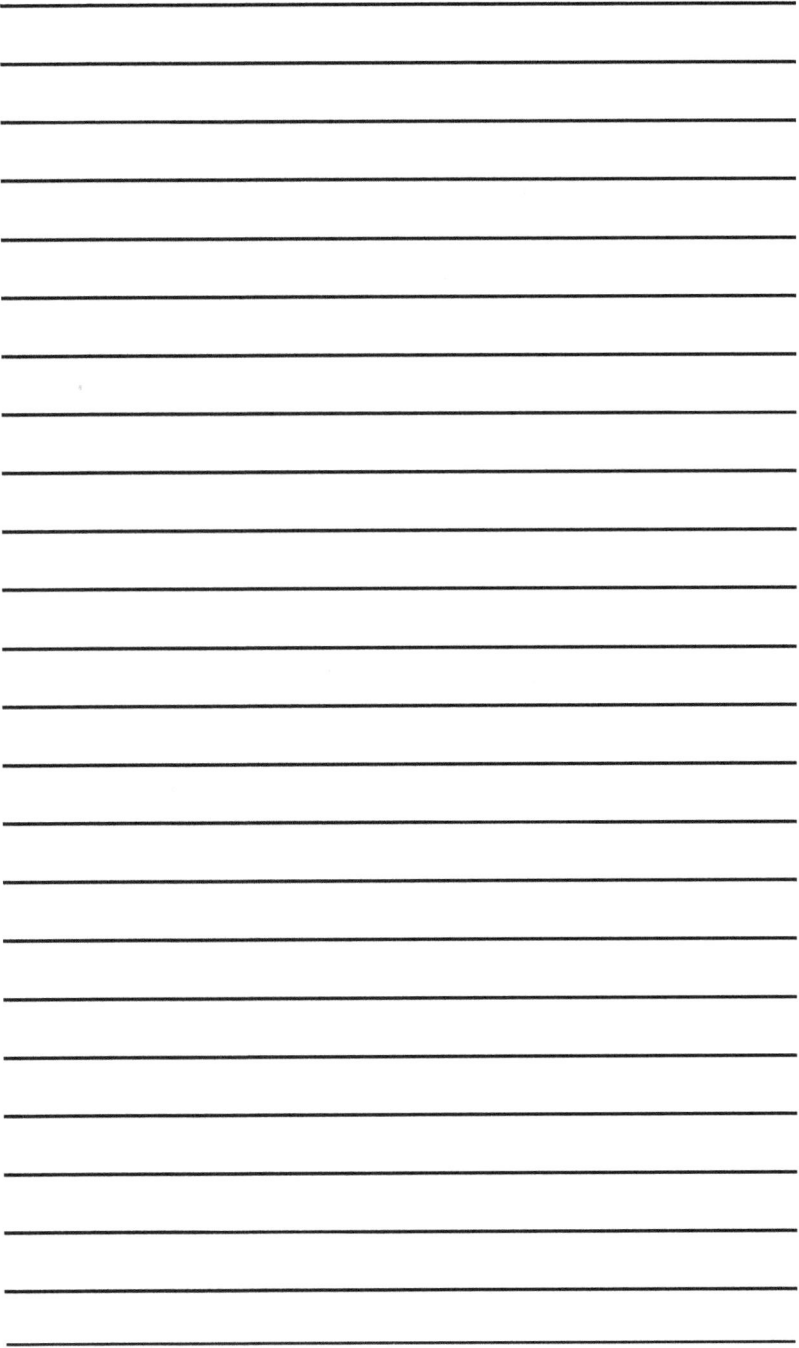

SPIRITUAL BELIEFS

(Faith, Worship, and Prayer)

We all have a belief system that has shaped how and what we believe. Often those are grounded in how we were raised or in learning and study as an adult. It is important that couples discuss their belief systems to decide if they are committed to living with each other's spiritual and other beliefs.

Answer and Discuss.

Do I know my spiritual beliefs?
Discuss thoughts about God/Jesus, faith, worship, the Bible, religion, and prayer.

Do I know and respect my mate's spiritual beliefs?

Do I have a faith story?
Share and discuss the story or lack thereof.

Do I believe in or value community worship?
Share and discuss if you will worship together or okay with separate worship and faith experiences.

Do I believe in worship in the home and its significance?

Do I know if prayer and study of the Holy Scriptures will be a regular part of our life together? Plan how and how often you will incorporate this into your marriage.

SPIRITUAL BELIEFS – WHAT IS OUR PLAN?

_____

_____

_____

_____

_____

_____

_____

_____

_____

_____

_____

_____

_____

_____

_____

_____

_____

_____

_____

_____

_____

VISION

Proverbs 29:18 talks about people perishing without a vision. This can also be applied to other aspects of life, including marriage. Many things can distract couples from what is important. A vision allows you to stay focused on your love and covenant commitment.

Answer and Discuss.

Do I value the idea or agree that a marriage should have a vision? If not, discuss what shapes your view.

Do I have a vision for my marriage?
Consider what you would like your marriage to represent in your family, community, and world and the love legacy you want to live and leave.

Do I understand the importance of my mate and I having a unified vision? Consider writing the vision in the form of a vision statement and framing it nicely to hang in your home.

Do I know if my parents' marriage, or lack thereof, shaped my view and vision of marriage?

Do I have marriage goals that will position our love and relationship for growth?

VISION — WHAT IS OUR PLAN?

SPEAKING SPIRIT

Words matter. I was taught that words cannot hurt you, and I firmly believe that we should not let what other people say control us or cause negative views of ourselves. However, hurtful words can have a devastating effect on emotions. Even the Bible tells us that evil words spoken from the heart can defile a person (Matthew 15:18). In your relationship, choose your words carefully. Keep your heart pure, filled with respect, love, and grace because that will dictate how you communicate. How you communicate can make or break your marriage.

Answer and Discuss.

Do I know my love language and how I best process information?

Do I know my mate's love language and how she/he best processes information? Take extra time here. It is critical to know how you want to be approached and communicated with: timing, mood, and how you process information are key to successful communication. If you are not familiar with love languages, read "The Five Love Languages" by Gary Chapman.

Do I give my mate compliments often and speak well of her/him to others?

Do I take the time to engage my mate in meaningful conversation on a regular basis? Don't assume everything is well with your mate, ask.

Do I give constructive feedback (with positive language) and ask how I might support my mate? For example: "please listen" versus "be quiet" is positive.

Do I quickly say, "I'm Sorry?" Operate in the marriage so that you don't have to say this often, but because you are human, apologizing will inevitably become necessary at times.

SPEAKING SPIRIT — WHAT IS OUR PLAN?

_____

_____

_____

_____

_____

_____

_____

_____

_____

_____

_____

_____

_____

_____

_____

_____

_____

_____

_____

CHAPTER 2
EMOTIONAL

The Journey

Submission/Consideration

Affirmation

You have a beautiful soul. I feel it is one of the greatest mysteries of God's creation—the unknown place that houses your unique will and emotions and, at its core, makes you human. A lot has gone into forming and shaping your emotions (the great, the good, and the not-so-good). But wherever you are emotionally, know that Jesus has been there (having felt every emotion that you feel) and is more than able to strengthen your soul. And you will certainly need a strong soul to successfully coexist with another human being. This chapter deals with the importance of being emotionally connected with your mate.

Pray for strength and transformation through a renewed mind.

SCRIPTURE REFERENCES:

1 Corinthians 13:4-7

4) Love is patient, love is kind. It does not envy, it does not boast, it is not proud. 5) It does not dishonor others, it is not self-seeking, it is not easily angered, it keeps no record of wrongs. 6) Love does not delight in evil but rejoices with the truth. 7) It always protects, always trusts, always hopes, always perseveres.

Romans 12:2

2) Do not conform to the pattern of this world, but be transformed by the renewing of your mind. Then you will be able to test and approve what God's will is—his good, pleasing and perfect will.

Philippians 2:5

5) In your relationships with one another, have the same mindset as Christ Jesus:

Ephesians 5:21

21) Submit to one another out of reverence for Christ.

THE JOURNEY

The soul, emotions, and feelings are major areas to tackle when it comes to relationships. Take time to do serious soul searching. Be honest and open to understanding your own emotional journey and the emotional journey of your mate. But more importantly, be receptive and ready to change. It will not benefit the relationship to bring past negative thought processes and emotions to the union. You might need to apply the "Keep, Give, Throw Away" strategy: Keep what is productive, Give some to God to renew, and Throw out the old.

Answer and Discuss.

Do I know my psychological history and the psychological history of my mate? How has it shaped me as an adult? What is the psychological history of my family/my mate's family? Discuss whether you feel emotionally balanced. Are there psychological or mental health concerns that could potentially negatively affect the success of the marriage?

Do I know my emotional needs?

Do I know the emotional needs of my mate?

Do I care about and support those emotional needs? This goes deeper than knowing your love language. Take time to explore your emotional health and how it can be improved. Seek professional counseling, if needed.

Do I know and understand what it means to be emotionally present?

Discuss your thoughts about emotional intimacy. Be emotionally available to talk and listen to your mate, continue to flirt, and be tuned in to your mate's soul so that you readily identify her/his emotions. To do this, you must not be chronically stressed out, preoccupied with work or other matters, worried, angry, or nonchalant. Together, develop a plan for how your marriage will not fall prey to the negative effects of constant stress or other distractions.

THE JOURNEY — WHAT IS OUR PLAN?

_____

_____

_____

_____

_____

_____

_____

_____

_____

_____

_____

_____

_____

_____

_____

_____

_____

_____

_____

_____

SUBMISSION/CONSIDERATION

You might be thinking, "Submission, really?" Yes, really! I know some people do not like that word when it comes to relationships, especially in terms of the wife submitting to the husband. But submitting is not about control. It is about respect and consideration, and it is not one-sided - each mate should submit to the other. Let your mutual love and care for your mate override traditional views about submission.

Answer and Discuss.

Do I submit to my mate?

Think about your mate's leadership, good qualities, and value she/he brings, such as the ability to make wise decisions. If your mate is submitted to the divine leadership of God and His ways, that positions you under God's leadership. That is a win-win-win for the marriage.

Do I view my mate as my Queen/King?

Think about submission from the perspective of her/his value as a person, uniqueness, and royal qualities. Discuss what this means for the relationship and how it might enhance the marriage.

Do I know when to let go of my ego and place more value on how my mate feels?

Do I control my mate or make her/him feel inferior or trapped?

SUBMISSION/CONSIDERATION — WHAT IS OUR PLAN?

AFFIRMATION

My definition of "affirmation" is to make a positive statement that encourages and causes a feeling of security and strength. Speaking affirmations daily is important for both individuals and the relationship. Affirmations will breathe life into your marriage and help keep the focus on your mate's strengths and value. Think about what initially attracted you to each other and the growth you have seen in your mate. In areas that challenge her/him, encourage your mate with delicacy, care, and practical options.

Answer and Discuss.

Do I affirm my mate on a regular basis? How? If not, why not?

Am I uncomfortable affirming my mate? Why? Discuss ways to increase affirming your mate.

Do I know my mate's strengths and areas of challenge?

Think about how your strengths complement your mate's challenges. Think about your challenges and how you can overcome them.

Here is a list of suggested affirmations. Finish the sentences based on how you feel about your mate. Develop your own list.

I love you more than :

_____

_____

I love that you

_____

_____

You are so

_____

_____

You have a strength that

_____

_____

I care that you are

_____

_____

You are my

_____

_____

Our love

_____

_____

No matter what, we

_____

_____

I love you. I am in love with you

_____

_____

AFFIRMATION — WHAT IS OUR PLAN?

_____

_____

_____

_____

_____

_____

_____

_____

_____

_____

_____

_____

_____

_____

_____

_____

_____

_____

CHAPTER 3

FRIENDSHIP

The "Like" Factor

Trust

Cohabitation

I cannot imagine life without true, close friends whose compatibility and connection with me are a source of power and strength that energizes the relationship through both good and challenging times. Friends talk, listen, laugh, cry, and share everything. Even when miles apart, friends still feel close. Does this describe you and your mate? This chapter deals with the importance of friendship in marriage and how it is the lifeline of a successful relationship. Pray for your mate and the blessing of an even stronger friendship bond.

SCRIPTURE REFERENCES:

Job 16:5

5) But my mouth would encourage you; comfort from my lips would bring you relief.

Proverbs 17:17a

17) A friend loves at all times.

Proverbs 27: 9b-10

9b)…The pleasantness of a friend springs from their heartfelt advice. 10) Do not forsake your friend or a friend of your family, and do not go to your relative's house when disaster strikes you—better a neighbor nearby than a relative far away.

Ecclesiastes 4:9-10a, 12b

9) Two are better than one, because they have a good return for their labor: 10) If either of them falls down, one can help the other up.
12b) A cord of three strands is not quickly broken. *(God, Husband, Wife)*

John 15:12-13

12) My command is this: Love each other as I have loved you. 13) Greater love has no one than this: to lay down one's life for one's friends.

THE "LIKE" FACTOR

I once heard a married woman say of her husband: "I love him, but I don't like him." It was a disheartening reality that might have resulted from years of negative, personal outcomes from her mate. The "like" factor includes liking the person's spirit, character, personality, how she/he honors you, speaks to you, treats you, makes you feel; it could include liking her/his spiritual strength and love for Christ, leadership, demeanor, wisdom, smile, positive outlook on life, intellect, humor, tenacity, and the list goes on. Yes, there will be times when you do not like your mate's non-personal actions, like when she/he leaves clothes on the floor - that is perfectly normal and not part of the "like" factor. I know you love your mate, but I hope you like her/him just as much.

Answer and Discuss.

Do I like my mate? What does that mean to me?
What specific characteristics do I like about my mate?

Do I enjoy my mate's company? In what way?

Do I know that I will be my mate's friend for life, even when she/he might disappoint me?

Do I know the importance of becoming more likable to my mate over the span of the relationship?

Imagine waking up fifteen years into the marriage and saying to your mate, "I don't like you." What changes or challenges in your mate could have contributed to this? Discuss specific actions needed to become more likable to your mate over time.

THE "LIKE" FACTOR — WHAT IS OUR PLAN?

_____

_____

_____

_____

_____

_____

_____

_____

_____

_____

_____

_____

_____

_____

_____

_____

_____

_____

_____

_____

_____

TRUST

"I believe you." "I can consistently count on you." "Thank you for always being honest." These are just a few statements that I feel are key to establishing trust in a relationship. Trust in a marriage is on the hierarchy with love and is equally essential. Consistent patterns of open, honest communication and actions earn trust.

Answer and Discuss.

Do I trust my mate 100%?

Do I have secrets that could potentially harm the marriage or negatively affect how I interact with my mate? If there are gaps in trust, discuss how you got there. List specific steps to close the gaps and move forward. Always be upfront and honest.

Do I agree that we are a team and have a trusted partnership? Discuss how this shows up in your partnership and ways to grow trust. You both are MVP's (most valuable persons) and should have equal skin in the game.

Do I say "we/us" more than "I/me" and offer ongoing positive experiences for my mate in my communication and actions?

Do I always tell my mate the truth, even when it's uncomfortable? Am I open to hearing the truth from my mate?

Discuss how you will handle times when trust might be compromised. Make sure in hard conversations, you communicate with respect, care, love, and grace.

Do I have a trusted accountability partner to occasionally share my joys and concerns, someone who will listen and give godly, honest, constructive feedback? Always talk to God and your partner first, but this is a trusted friend, pastor, or professional therapist. Make a list of potential candidates.

TRUST – WHAT IS OUR PLAN?

_____

_____

_____

_____

_____

_____

_____

_____

_____

_____

_____

_____

_____

_____

_____

_____

_____

_____

_____

_____

COHABITATION

Sharing personal space with another human being can be quite challenging. Personal habits and preferences for how things are organized or kept can cause tremendous anxiety in a marriage if there is not understanding and negotiation up front. Respect for your mate's preferences is vital, and compromise is going to be necessary. In some instances, you might want to discuss what is at the core of some of your habits and be open to change.

Answer and Discuss.

Do I know what the deal breakers are when it comes to sharing space with my mate? Discuss why these are important to you.

Do I consider myself organized or messy when it comes to housekeeping? Discuss what is at the root of these behaviors.

Do I respect my mate's time? Discuss any time management issues.

Do I have Obsessive-Compulsive Disorder (OCD) or OCD tendencies? OCD is linked to anxiety and uncontrollable, repetitive behaviors? If so, discuss what you think is the root cause, and develop strategies for alleviating the behaviors. Seek professional help, if needed.

Do I respect my mate's cohabitation preferences and work to find solutions when we face cohabitation issues? Discuss deal breakers and preferences that are negotiable.

Discuss how you will work as a partnership regarding household matters (decorating, cooking, dining, laundry, cleaning, trash, yardwork, etc.).

Discuss who will take the lead in ensuring that you both never go to bed angry. Someone must take ownership of leading this effort so that matters don't linger and grow. Maybe think about rotating the lead periodically so that one person does not feel overly burdened.

COHABITATION — WHAT IS OUR PLAN?

CHAPTER 4

PHYSICAL

Attraction/Beauty

Dating

The Reality of Change

Physical attributes are the most common initial attractor, but physical attraction goes much deeper than first catching the eye of a mate: in fact, it is a key component of maintaining a successful marriage, even when physical attributes change. This chapter gets saucy! It deals with physical intimacy and some components to keeping a healthy, physical relationship. As you read this chapter, keep in mind what initially attracted you to your mate.

SCRIPTURE REFERENCES:
(EXCERPTS FROM SONG OF SOLOMON):

1:2-3a

Let him kiss me with the kisses of his mouth—for your love is more delightful than wine. Pleasing is the fragrance of your perfumes; your name is like perfume poured out.

1:13

My beloved is to me a sachet of myrrh resting between my breasts.

1:15a,16

How beautiful you are, my darling! Oh, how beautiful! . . . How handsome you are, my beloved! Oh, how charming!

2:14b

Let me hear your voice; for your voice is sweet, and your face is lovely.

3:1-4b

All night long on my bed, I looked for the one my heart loves; I looked for him but did not find him. I will get up now and go about the city, through its streets and squares; I will search for the one my heart loves. So I looked for him but did not find him.

The watchmen found me as they made their rounds in the city. "Have you seen the one my heart loves?" Scarcely had I passed them when I found the one my heart loves. I held him and would not let him go.

4:3a

Your lips are like a scarlet ribbon; your mouth is lovely.

4:5

Your breasts are like two fawns, like twin fawns of a gazelle that browse among the lilies.

4:9

You have stolen my heart . . . you have stolen my heart.

ATTRACTION AND BEAUTY

Only an individual can truly define what beauty means to her or him. Whatever the case, physical attributes most often initially catch one's attention—gorgeous eyes, beautiful smile, alluring walk or "Obama-like" swag, hair texture, sweet or bass voice, curves, well-manicured feet, and anything else you may find attractive. Whatever it was for you, hold on to it; that feeling can always be used to ignite more attraction.

Answer and Discuss.

Do I know my mate's sexual and medical history?

Do I want to share my sexual and medical history? Discuss sexual and medical conditions that should be revealed.

Do I flirt with my mate? Am I receptive to my mate's flirting (like it, enjoy it, respond positively)? Flirting should be often and genuine. It can be vocal or physical. It does not necessarily mean sex will follow. Sometimes flirt just because. Do not ever make your mate feel bad about flirting. Discuss likes and dislikes.

Do I make intentional efforts to maintain a healthy, sexy body?

Sexy does not mean you are a small size or have no physical flaws - you and your mate should define what is sexy and work together to be sexy and healthy for each other. Discuss practical ways to do this.

Do I place more attention on my mate's outer beauty or inner beauty? Discuss her/his outer and inner qualities and the beauty they bring to you and the relationship.

Do I know how often I require or prefer physical intimacy or sex?

Do I smile when I think of my mate or light up when she/he walks in the room? Base this on your mate's spirit and soul, not situations.

ATTRACTION/BEAUTY — WHAT IS OUR PLAN?

DATING

Okay, put on your memory shoes and let's take a walk down memory lane: Remember all those good times when you and your mate were dating? I see you smiling. It should not stop when you get married. Over time some dynamics will change, especially if you have children, but you must continue to date consistently to keep your spiritual, emotional, and physical connection AND to keep the romance hot!

Answer and Discuss.

Do I know that dating is essential in marriage and must be intentional and consistent? Define what dating means to you.

It is not necessarily about sex, leaving the house, or spending money. Whether you date for one hour per week or an entire weekend, it is all about connection.

Do I hug or touch my mate daily? This is necessary in the marriage and is not necessarily about sex. As humans, we need physical touch. As a married couple, you need it even more to stay connected. Hug often. If you are not a hugger or do not like human touch (or have had bad experiences), discuss it with your mate and seek therapy from a professional, if needed.

Do I know what I like in dating activities?

Do I know what my mate likes? Make a list of dating activities that you enjoy. Decide how often will be the date days/nights. I suggest at least two dates per week: one in the home and one outside the home. Both mates should plan one per week. Make a monthly calendar, and keep it visible. Sometimes simple activities provide the most fun.

Do I have a plan for keeping the romance hot and sizzling? Be open to trying new and different actions; and do not let age be a hindrance. There are always creative ways to connect.

DATING — WHAT IS OUR PLAN?

THE REALITY OF CHANGE

Look at an old photo of yourself. Guess what? Your physical qualities have changed. They will continue to change. Regardless of the number and quality of beauty enhancements, aging does not stop. I hope physical beauty is not the major reason you are marrying your partner, rather for her/his inner beauty and spirit-soul.

Answer and Discuss.

Do I know how my mate generally deals with change?

Do I have major concerns about aging?

Do I stay committed and faithful to my mate and marriage despite physical or mental changes? Examples: weight gain/loss, medical conditions, mental illness, paralysis, loss of hearing/speech/sight, etc.

Do I know that, as much as possible, I should manage change by taking care of my spirit, mind, and body? What wellness goals do you have in each of these areas? List specific ways to collaborate with your mate on physical and mental wellness goals, such as regular professional counseling and exercising together.

Do I know my mate's expectations in the case of major changes in physical or mental capabilities? Discuss care giving, support systems, remaining faithful, support groups, etc.

THE REALITY OF CHANGE — WHAT IS OUR PLAN?

_____

_____

_____

_____

_____

_____

_____

_____

_____

_____

_____

_____

_____

_____

_____

_____

_____

_____

_____

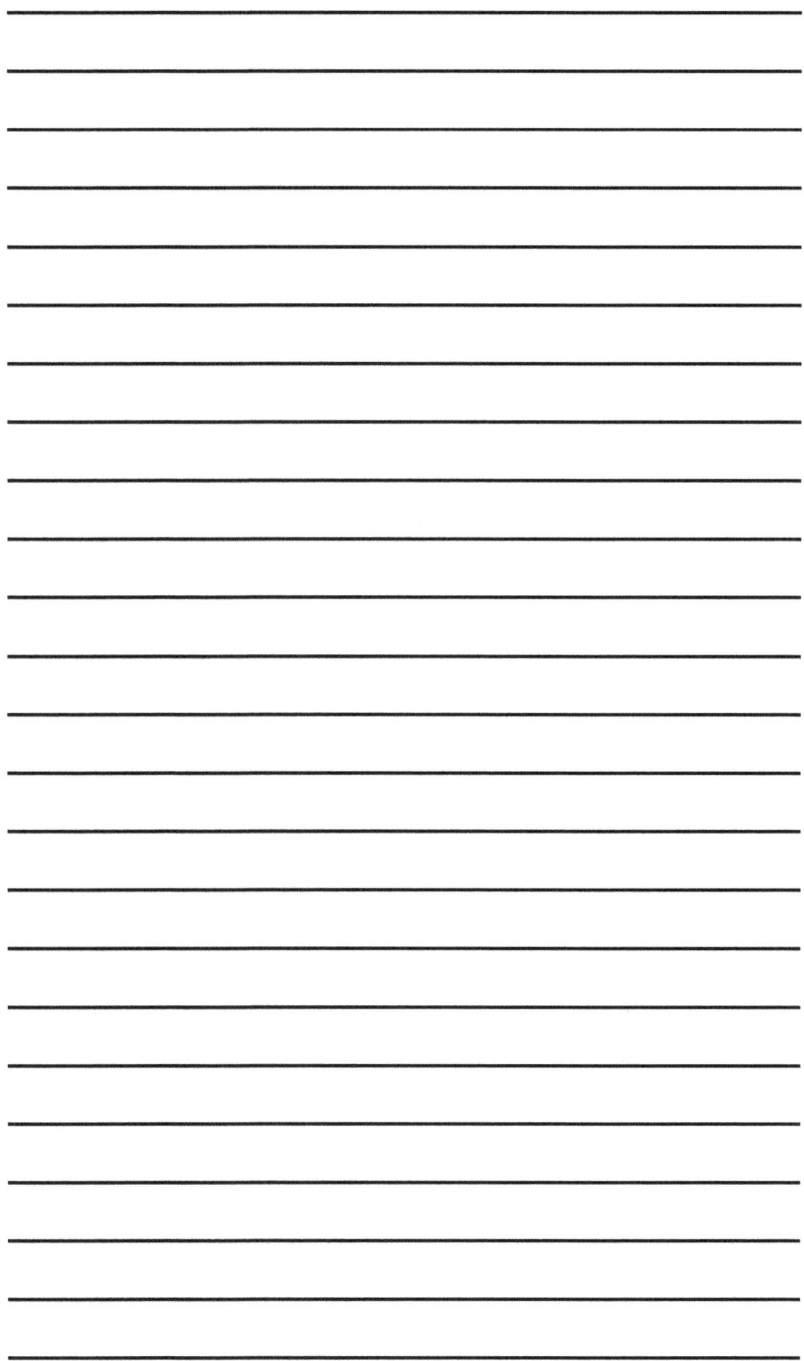

CHAPTER 5

FUN

Freedom

Laughter

Bucket List

It is important to have wholesome fun as an individual and as a couple. It is one of the most important investments for a successful relationship and marriage. Fun could be a no-cost activity like playing pillow fight in bed, something carefree like solving a puzzle together, or even fulfilling those bucket list dreams. When you invest in fun together, it will yield rewards of freedom, joy, and a lot of laughs. No pun intended but have fun with this chapter! Put on some of your favorite music or go to one of your favorite spots as you delve into the questions and discussion here.

SCRIPTURE REFERENCES:

Exodus 15:20

20) . . . and all the women followed her, with timbrels and dancing.

Deuteronomy 14:26

26) . . . Then you and your household shall eat there in the presence of the LORD your God and rejoice.

Ecclesiastes 3:4

4) . . . time to laugh . . . time to dance . . .

Psalms 118:24 (KJV)

24) This is the day the Lord has made. We will rejoice and be glad in it.

Proverbs 17:22

22) A cheerful heart is good medicine . . .

Luke 2:42

42) . . . they went up to the festival.

FREEDOM

One of the reasons I did not combine the dating and fun chapters is that I feel it is important for a married person to maintain some sense of individuality and personal freedom. Being married does not mean you cease to be yourself or engage in personal activities. Some questions below focus on individual freedom and your partner's view on it. I believe that only when you are free as an individual can you come together and enjoy healthy freedom as a couple.

Answer and Discuss.

Do I understand that my mate, as an individual, needs personal time and hobbies that are unique to her/him? If not, discuss the experience (or experiences) that has shaped your view or insecurities.

Do I encourage and support individuality and creativity in my mate? Why or why not?

Do I know the fun activities that I like and that my mate likes? List them and discuss why they are fun for you and how you started pursuing these activities.

Do I understand what it means to be "free" or to have freedom in a relationship/marriage? Discuss this from the perspective of trust, respect, and admiration.

Do I have unresolved trauma or trust issues that might hinder my sense of freedom or courage to be my authentic self?

FREEDOM – WHAT IS OUR PLAN?

LAUGHTER

The Bible makes many references to laughter and how it is good for the soul, much like medicine. There are many statistics and scientific studies showing the benefits of laughter. Laughing therapy was made popular years ago. Even if there were no statistics or studies, you know that when you laugh, you feel good, you are energized, and you just darn feel better. An article published in Forbes a couple of years ago stated that "couples who laugh together report having higher -quality relationships." I hope that you have shared many laughs and will continue to do so.

Answer and Discuss.

Do I remember the first laugh or first memorable laugh I shared with my mate? Share your memory with her/him.

Do I like to laugh? Does my mate like to laugh? If not, discuss the experience (or experiences) that has shaped your view and if you are open to therapy to help incorporate more laughter into your life.

Do I understand the importance of laughing with my mate and its positive effects on our relationship? Discuss this importance.

Do I know my laughing triggers? Name some.

Do I know my mate's qualities, habits, and quirks that bring me joy?

Reminisce about some good laughs you have shared, especially the gut-wrenching ones.

LAUGHTER — WHAT IS OUR PLAN?

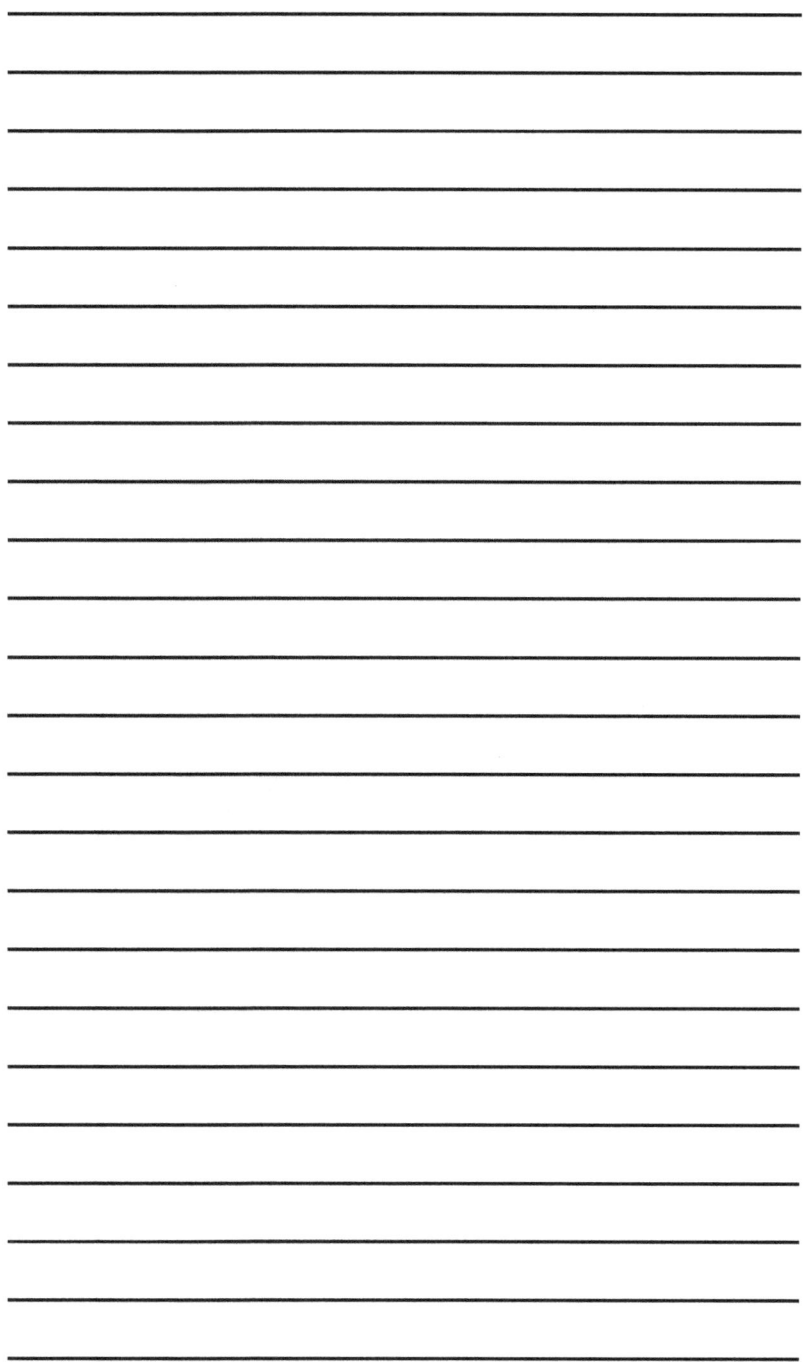

BUCKET LIST

A bucket list is a list of things you would like to do before you "kick the bucket." It sounds a little morbid but making a bucket list is incredibly energizing and therapeutic. Focus on your desires, the great accomplishments you will achieve, dream adventures, and fun places you will visit. There is no limit to how long or short your list must be, so have fun with this part of planning your lives together.

Answer and Discuss.

Do I feel personal bucket lists/dreams/goals are important? If not, share with your mate what shaped your feelings.

Do I like adventure? If safety or cost were not issues, what adventures would you like to experience?

Do I have a bucket list? Does my mate have one?
If so, share the list and why you would like to do these things.

Do I understand the importance of married couples having shared dreams in a relationship? If not, discuss with your mate what has shaped your view and if you are open to changing for the success of the relationship.

Spend time discussing and planning dream accomplishments and adventures.

BUCKET LIST – WHAT IS OUR PLAN?

_____

_____

_____

_____

_____

_____

_____

_____

_____

_____

_____

_____

_____

_____

_____

_____

_____

_____

_____

_____

CHAPTER 6

FINANCIAL

Your Money Story

Budget

Wealth Plan

It is extremely important for couples to be financially sound and to have a workable, financial plan before saying "I Do." This applies to all levels of income: whether great or small, a plan is necessary! Lack of financial planning is one of the major causes of marital problems and divorce. Even if other aspects of the relationship are flourishing, financial stress can quickly cause a downward spiral.

SCRIPTURE REFERENCES:

Proverbs 13:22

22) A good person leaves an inheritance for their children's children.

Proverbs 31:16-20, 24

16) She considers a field and buys it; out of her earnings she plants a vineyard.

17) She sets about her work vigorously; her arms are strong for her tasks.

18) She sees that her trading is profitable, and her lamp does not go out at night.

19) In her hand she holds the distaff and grasps the spindle with her fingers.

20) She opens her arms to the poor and extends her hands to the needy.

24) She makes linen garments and sells them, and supplies the merchants with sashes.

YOUR MONEY STORY

Your money story started the day you were born. It is rooted in the economic status of the person(s) who raised you and how finances were handled in the household. Something as simple as putting pennies in a piggy bank taught you the importance of saving. It is possible that as an adult, you have educated yourself on responsible money matters, but underlying feelings about saving, investing, paying bills, etc. are nevertheless somewhat connected to the role money played in your upbringing.

Answer and Discuss.

Do I know my money story? Think about your childhood:

● Was money talked about in the home? What were you taught about the value of money, saving, spending, etc.?

● Did your parent(s) struggle to meet basic needs like food and clothing, or was money not an issue?

● Were you paid to do chores? Were you required to save a portion of the payment? Did you have a piggy bank?

● Did you hear your parent(s) discuss tithing, other spiritual giving concepts, or giving to charity?

● Did you often hear your parents argue about financial matters?

● When were you introduced to the idea of buying on credit or using credit cards?

Do I understand how these childhood influences affect how I handle money as an adult? What positive and negative effects linger or need to change to improve my financial situation?

Do I know my mate's money story? Ask her/him to share based on the bullet points above.

Think about mindset and practical changes that need to happen in you in order to have a successful financial life in the marriage.

MONEY STORY — WHAT IS OUR PLAN?

BUDGET

Yep, the dreaded "B" word that most people do not want to talk about! A budget is a financial guide for money coming in (income) and monies going out (expenses). Some call it a spending plan because it is a plan for how money is spent. It is a valuable resource for tracking finances and a necessary tool regardless of how much or how little you make.

Answer and Discuss.

Do I understand how to budget? If not, am I willing to learn?

Do I currently live on a budget or have a spending plan? How successful am I at managing a budget? Is a budget helpful to my life and livelihood?

Do I know if my partner lives on a budget or has a spending plan?

Do I have issues with my partner's spending habits?

Do I know my partner's financial history, net worth, savings, and investments? How important is this to me? Are there any deal breakers?

Do I know my partner's debt ratio and credit score? How important is this to me? Are there any deal breakers?

BUDGET – WHAT IS OUR PLAN?

Sample Budget Worksheet

A sample **Budget Worksheet** is attached. Spend time discussing if you will combine incomes and expenses, how household finances will be handled, and how you will stay accountable to the budget and to each other in financial matters.

Monthly income for the month of: _____

Item	Amount
Salary	
Spouse's salary	
Dividends	
Interest	
Investments	
Reimbursements	
Other	
Total	

Monthly expenses for the month of: _____ _____

Item	Amount
Bills	
Groceries	
Mortgage	
Credit Card	
Gas	
IRA	
Laundry	
Car loan	
Utilities	
Clothing	
Daycare	
Medical/Dental	
Household	
Savings	
Property Taxes	
Other	
Total	

Income vs. Expenses

Item	Amount
Monthly income	
Monthly expenses	
Difference	

BUDGET NOTES

WEALTH PLAN

You just spent a considerable amount of time planning a budget, which is necessary for the daily, weekly, and monthly success of your household finances. Now, we will shift the focus to something long-term: wealth. I used to think wealth was only for certain people until I learned that we all have potential and opportunities to build beyond making and spending money. Wealth is the gift that keeps giving, even after we leave this life—a financial legacy passed on to children, family, or charitable purposes. It has the potential to help make the world a better place.

Answer and Discuss.

Do I understand wealth? What is my definition or view of wealth?

Do I have generational wealth or currently have a wealth plan?

Do I know if my partner is wealthy? If so, am I marrying for her/his wealth?

Do I want to build wealth with my mate? Do I have a wealth plan?

Consider meeting with a trusted financial advisor to learn about options.

Do I know the financial legacy I want to leave?

Think about real estate, businesses, investments, assets, and planned giving.

Do I know to whom I want to leave my wealth?

Do I have a Will or planning to develop one soon?

WEALTH PLAN – WHAT IS OUR PLAN?

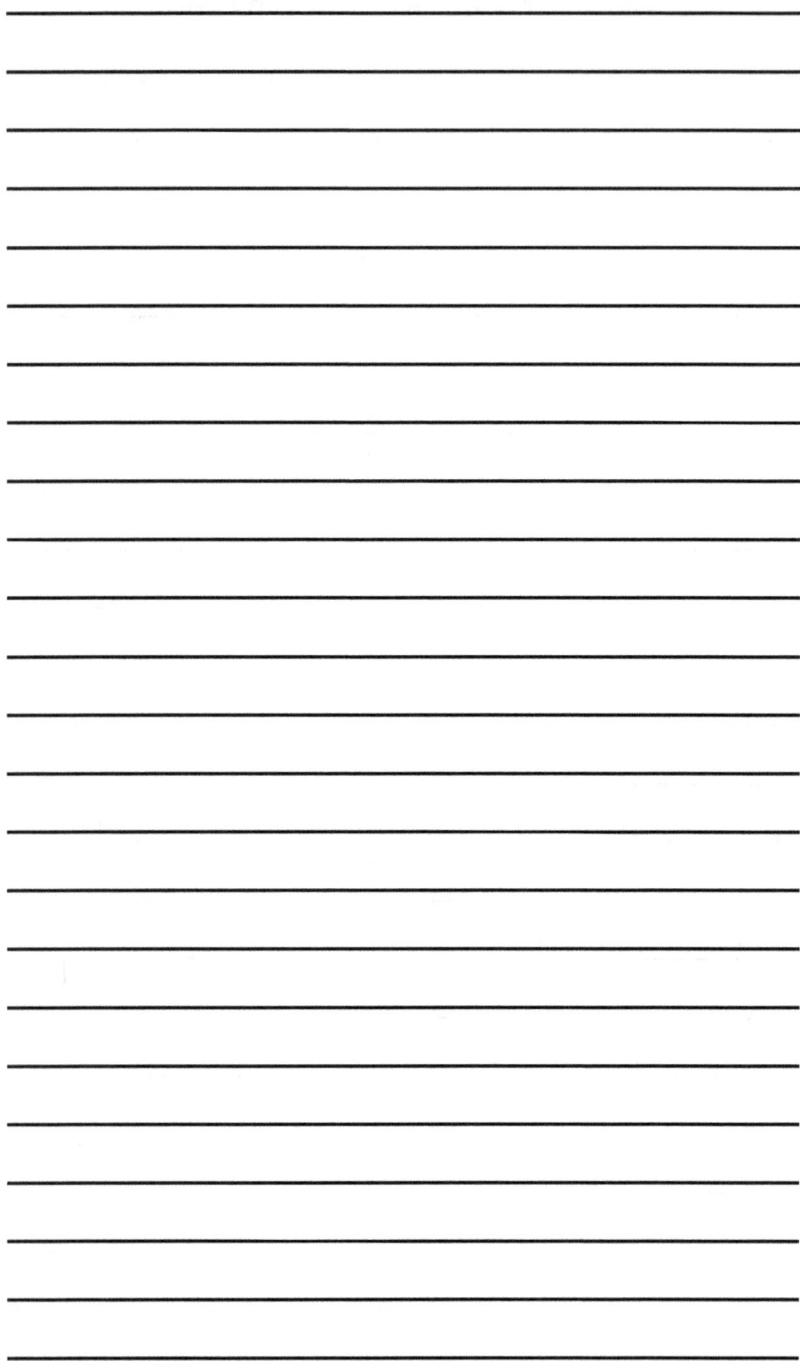

CHAPTER 7

FAMILY

Our Families

Children

Family Unity

Family is a God-ordained unit and is critical to the fiber of our world. Family values and ideologies influence who we are and shape our moral compass. Fortunately or unfortunately, we do not choose our biological family: two people come together intimately, and the chain begins. For some, that is a blessing; for others, it can be a challenge.

Whatever the dynamics in your families, it is crucial that together you decide expectations and boundaries. For the purposes of answering the questions in this chapter, "family" is made up of your mate's children, parents, and siblings.

SCRIPTURE REFERENCES:

Exodus 20:12

12) "Honor your father and your mother, so that you may live long in the land the LORD your God is giving you.

Psalms 127:3-5

3) Children are a heritage from the LORD, offspring a reward from him.

4) Like arrows in the hands of a warrior are children born in one's youth.

5) Blessed is the man whose quiver is full of them.

Zechariah 8:5

5) The city streets will be filled with boys and girls playing there.

Luke 2:39-40

39) When Joseph and Mary had done everything required by the Law of the Lord, they returned to Galilee to their own town of Nazareth. 40) And the child grew and became strong.

OUR FAMILIES

When two people decide to marry, it is a decision that affects their families. Relationships on both sides must be established. The ideal situation is that both families will instantly connect and operate as a big, happy family! Unfortunately, that is not the case in many families. Hopefully, you have met your mate's family, and you all get along well. If not, you will have to decide how to move forward so that your marriage is not negatively affected by family tension.

Answer and Discuss.

Do I know my mate's relationship and history with her/his family?

Discuss with your mate any of her/his family dynamics that could potentially cause tension in the marriage.

Do I understand the importance of healthy relationships with my mate's family? If this is not important to you, discuss why not. If it is not important to her/him, are you okay with that?

Do I know or have I met my mate's family?
Discuss your experience and thoughts.

Do I like my mate's family? Why or why not?

Do I have extended or blended family that will be a regular part of our home life? What joys or concerns do you have about the arrangement?

Do I have deal breakers or concerns about my mate's family that I need to discuss with my mate?

Discuss expectations and boundaries for each of your families.

OUR FAMILIES — WHAT IS OUR PLAN?

_____

_____

_____

_____

_____

_____

_____

_____

_____

_____

_____

_____

_____

_____

_____

_____

_____

_____

_____

_____

_____

_____

CHILDREN

Children are a blessing from God. They are often referred to as "bundles of joy," which is quite appropriate. We gain much joy from their innocent existence. However, there can be challenges in having and raising children, as there can be in any relationship. If you decide that children will be part of your lives, crucial planning will be necessary for their development and well-being and to establish how you will successfully function as a family unit.

Answer and Discuss.

Do I like the idea of birthing or having children? Does my mate like the idea of having children? If not, discuss what influenced your decision.

Do I have dependent children?

Do I want children or want to have more children? What shaped this decision? Does my mate have dependent children? Does my mate want children or more children? What shaped her/his decision?

Do I know the average yearly cost of child expenses? Determine if cost is a factor in the decision to have children.

Do I know how many children I want?

Do I know how many children my mate wants?

Do I know how we will reward good behavior?

Do I know how we will handle discipline?

Do I know who will be the primary disciplinarian or if we will share responsibilities?

Do I know if we will home-school or use public or private school? Consider pros, cons, and options.

Do I know how we might handle major medical issues with our child or children, like a life-threatening chronic illness?

CHILDREN — WHAT IS OUR PLAN?

_____

_____

_____

_____

_____

_____

_____

_____

_____

_____

_____

_____

_____

_____

_____

_____

_____

_____

_____

_____

FAMILY UNITY

For the purposes of this section, discuss family unity in terms of your immediate family who live in the same household.

"Unit" is the root word of unity. In order to be a family unit, there has to be unity. It does not necessarily mean agreement but has more to do with respect, common vision, shared mindset and goals. Family unity, or the lack thereof, can determine the fate of the family. There is a popular saying, "a family that prays together stays together." I certainly believe prayer will strengthen the family bond. There are also other practical ways to enhance family unity. Let's talk about them.

Answer and Discuss.

Do I understand the importance of family unity?

What does that mean to me and how does it tie to growth of the marriage?

Do I have a vision for how our family will function and grow as a unit in love, care, and support of one another?

Do I have suggested family goals? If not, brainstorm and jot down some goals to discuss with your mate.

Do I have thoughts about compromise as it relates to initiating, maintaining, and strengthening the family bond? If not, brainstorm and jot down notes to discuss with your mate.

Do I have thoughts about family rules and rewards/consequences for following/breaking rules? If not, brainstorm and jot down notes to discuss with your mate.

Do I have thoughts about the term "agree to disagree" and how it might respectfully settle compromise in family discussions.

FAMILY UNITY — WHAT IS OUR PLAN?

CONCLUSION

Do I?

I hope you do.

If you are ready to say "I Do", I am overjoyed and excited for you and your mate, congratulations!

You have done the work and taken the time to ask, answer, discuss, and plan in seven important areas: spiritual, emotional, friendship, physical, fun, financial , and family to bring you to your decision. Now you have a wedding to plan! Periodically review and refine your marriage plans, and continue to do the work to grow together.

If you are single and not engaged, my prayer is that you are now better equipped to make an informed decision when the time comes. I applaud your courage to open your heart to this process and to complete the book. Self-assessment and introspection can be quite challenging, but hopefully it has been worth the time.

If you are engaged and have decided to pause wedding plans to wait on God or other reasons, I honor your wisdom and decision. God is with you. He will guide you, give you strength, and provide answers. Use this waiting period to continue seeking God, increase time with Him, and listen for His voice. Also, keep discovering who you are and what you want in a mate and in life. Surround yourself with trusted, like-minded friends who will inspire you to grow and be your best self.

If you are married and used this book to reassess your commitment, carry on in the spirit of the eagle: soar to higher heights in love and life.

Blessings, Love and Light,

Janice

www.ingramcontent.com/pod-product-compliance
Lightning Source LLC
Chambersburg PA
CBHW050733030426
42336CB00012B/1547